The 5 Minute Procrastination Addiction Cure

Eliminating Procrastination By Starting In 5 Minutes Or Less

The 5 Minute Self Help series (Book 1)

Magnus Muller

Text Copyright © Magnus Muller

All rights reserved. No part of this guide may be reproduced in any form without permission in writing from the publisher except in the case of brief quotations embodied in critical articles or reviews.

Legal & Disclaimer

The information contained in this book and its contents is not designed to replace or take the place of any form of medical or professional advice; and is not meant to replace the need for independent medical, financial, legal or other professional advice or services, as may be required. The content and information in this book has been provided for educational and entertainment purposes only.

The content and information contained in this book has been compiled from sources deemed reliable, and it is accurate to the best of the Author's knowledge, information and belief. However, the Author cannot guarantee its accuracy and validity and cannot be held liable for any errors and/or omissions. Further, changes are periodically made to this book as and when needed. Where appropriate and/or necessary, you must consult a professional (including but not limited to your doctor, attorney, financial advisor or such other professional advisor) before using any of the suggested remedies, techniques, or information in this book.

Upon using the contents and information contained in this book, you agree to hold harmless the Author from and against any damages, costs, and expenses, including any legal fees potentially resulting from the application of any of the information provided by this book. This disclaimer applies to any loss, damages or injury caused by the use and application, whether directly or indirectly, of any advice or information presented, whether for breach of contract, tort, negligence, personal injury, criminal intent, or under any other cause of action.

You agree to accept all risks of using the information presented inside this book.

You agree that by continuing to read this book, where appropriate and/or necessary, you shall consult a professional (including but not limited to your doctor, attorney, or financial advisor or such other advisor as needed) before using any of the suggested remedies, techniques, or information in this book.

The 5 Minute Self Help Series

The 5 Minute Self Help Series (Book 1)

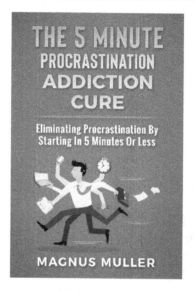

The 5 Minute Procrastination Addiction Cure
Eliminating Procrastination By Starting In 5 Minutes Or Less

By Magnus Muller

Kindle: http://www.amazon.com/dp/B07CT215ZZ
Paperback: http://www.amazon.com/dp/1983161640

The 5 Minute Self Help Series (Book 2)

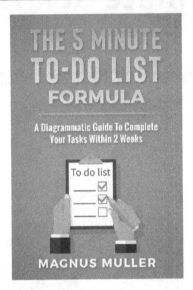

The 5 Minute To-Do List Formula
A Diagrammatic Guide To Complete Your Task Within 2 Weeks

By Magnus Muller

Kindle: http://www.amazon.com/dp/B07F8HFDLC
Paperback: http://www.amazon.com/dp/1983360260

The 5 Minute Self Help Series (Book 3)

The 5 Minute Mindfulness Practical Guide
20 Simple Habits To Lead A Stress Free Life, Reduce Anxiety And Treat Depression

By Magnus Muller

Kindle: http://www.amazon.com/dp/B07F8H6ZS2
Paperback: http://www.amazon.com/dp/1983360392

Author's message

Before I embarked on writing this book, I was previously also a procrastinator, just like you. I often delayed my tasks and in the end felt regretful for not completing them. I have tried to get rid of my procrastination, through reading numerous books and online articles, but mostly the strategies provided didn't work out for me.

One day, I came across this simple solution (which I call it the 5 minute solution) and implemented it. Ever since, this simple solution changed my life and now I am able to complete my daily tasks with ease just by following the simple instructions of this solution.

Hence, I have decided to write this short book, to help others that are like me; students and adults alike, to finally eliminate procrastination in the long run.

In this book, the 5 minute solution as well as the other tips that I am about to share with you are kept simple, concise and short as I myself know very well that for a procrastinator, one often end up procrastinating to even read finish extremely lengthy books.

Enjoy your read and I hope that after reading this book, you will be able to eliminate your inner procrastinator successfully and finally having more time freedom while completing all your tasks.

Table of Contents

The 5 Minute Self Help Series...5

Author's message..9

Introduction..13

Chapter 1: Why do people procrastinate?............17

Important things should not be procrastinated.........18

Understanding the mindset of procrastination..........19

The Monster of Panic: Why we can still finish our work when procrastinating...20

Why procrastination is dangerous, even if we can complete our tasks..21

The 5 consequences of procrastinating.....................22

Chapter 2: Procrastination- A bad habit.................27

How procrastination affects performance...................28

Why it is difficult to stop procrastinating....................30

Chapter 3: Tips to eliminate bad habits and create good ones..33

The 3 habits that you should nurture..........................34

Attacking the root of the problem...............................39

Chapter 4: The 5 minute solution............................45

The physics of real life..50

Chapter 5: Additional tips- A simple plan to overcome procrastination 55

Chapter 6: The 4 main benefits when you stop procrastinating 65

Conclusion 71

About the author 75

Leave a review 76

The 5 Minute Self Help Series 77

Check out other books 80

Introduction

Many of us have heard the term "procrastination", but not everyone is familiar with its actual meaning since it is not usually talked about. In fact, this word originated from Latin: "pro", meaning ahead, and "crastinus", referring to the future or postponement. In other words, procrastination is the action or habit of postponing tasks or activities that should be addressed and replacing them with other more pleasant ones, which may be less necessary or relevant.

In psychology, the term is defined as the feeling of anxiety before completing a task. It is a behavior disorder that affects most of us. We usually refer it to as "laziness" or say that someone is leaving things for tomorrow instead of doing them today.

It is indeed normal to suffer from procrastination occasionally, but there are some people who become "specialists" in procrastination. These people behave this way continuously because they somehow believe that tomorrow will be a more appropriate time to carry out any tasks they have to do. However, in reality, procrastination is a problem based on badly organizing time. If someone postpones or procrastinates something, this is clearly evasive behavior.

So, if you are someone who leaves things "for later", this book is for you. This book is aimed at students as well as adults and professionals who face the problem of procrastination in their everyday life. Fortunately, overcoming procrastination is easier than you think. We have a simple strategy that you can use as an effective tool at any time. Don't leave it for later—begin to overcome the procrastination in your life today. Imagine how many benefits you'll find if you end up reading just a few chapters of this book!

This book is a step-by-step guide on how to improve your habits and stop procrastinating. In each chapter, you'll find tips that you can implement in your life from today to overcome procrastination.

Enjoy!

Chapter 1: Why do people procrastinate?

It is extremely important to see the reason why people procrastinate. But let's break this down. We have already seen in the introduction that procrastination is an act of putting off anything that we could do now. At first glance, that doesn't seem like a big deal. You may even think this is something that is simply part of being human. However, the real problem is when this act of postponing is not occasional, but constant.

Whenever you sit down to work, do you feel the intense desire to check the fridge or turn on the TV? There is a scientific explanation behind this urge.

Even if you had never heard the word before (which would be difficult, since it has become a trendy word these days), we are all familiar with the idea of procrastination: that uncomfortable feeling throughout the body that makes you wait until the last minute before starting a university assignment, that impulse that tells you that now is a good time to watch an episode of a series that you just saw on TV, or simply the idea that you will start work once you have cleaned the entire house.

Important things should not be procrastinated

"Do not do today what can be left for tomorrow" is the motto of those who procrastinate; postpone as much as possible an important task that you know that you have to do, and you're really going to do it sooner or later. The main cause of procrastination seems to be the difficulty in adequately managing emotions—or rather, the misconception that in order to achieve something, we have to be motivated to do it.

Let's consider a familiar situation. A student was required to submit work a month prior to his admission into university. As a procrastinator, he constantly reminded himself: "The work is simple and I have a lot of time to spare. I just need to relax and be inspired before I start working on it." So, without realizing it, he ended up spending a good part of his time browsing the internet and meeting friends. Days and weeks passed, until suddenly it was the afternoon before the delivery date. He finally started his work, because he believed that he would work better under pressure, and by starting now rather than earlier he might produce something amazing.

Well, what makes the student decide to postpone his homework? Why does this behavior repeat again and again? Is it possible to stop procrastinating? These are some of the important questions that we would like to answer in this chapter and throughout this eBook. We aim to support everyone, not only students but also professionals and adults, so that they successfully develop their academic skills and achieve their career goals.

Understanding the mindset of procrastination

So, you may be wondering, why do we procrastinate? There are many areas that you can look at, but first let's understand how our minds work when we procrastinate.

Procrastination is the struggle between the limbic system and the prefrontal cortex of the brain. This may sound complicated, but it simply means that the limbic system (the part that contains the brain's pleasure center) fights with the prefrontal cortex (the part that is dedicated to planning things), and when the limbic system wins, you choose the task that gives you immediate satisfaction over one that would give you satisfaction in the long-term.

This means that your brain becomes addicted to procrastination, like anything else that generates dopamine. Dopamine modifies the neurons in your brain and makes you more likely to repeat the action that caused it.

Therefore, the main way to avoid procrastination is to be aware of what you do when you decide to procrastinate. Otherwise, you are allowing your limbic system to decide for you, and you know how that ends.

The Monster of Panic: Why we can still finish our work when procrastinating

But can the procrastinators never make any profit? Are they people unable to pass a test or deliver a job? The vast majority can, thanks to a mechanism that protects them: *the monster of panic.*

After a procrastinator falls into the spiral of activities that are as moderately pleasurable as absurd, they finally reach a point where there is almost no time to do their important tasks. Only at this point, when it is almost impossible to fix the mess, the monster of panic appears, scaring away the urge for instant gratification and forcing the procrastinator to finally focus on their necessary tasks.

The absurd situations caused by procrastinating are finally resolved at the last minute, thanks to our ability to maintain a state of extreme concentration and enormous capacity to work when we fall prey to panic: the panic of not delivering work on time, of failing a test... of failing in our responsibility.

This is the reason why we can still manage to complete all our work even at the last minute. All thanks to the monster of panic.

Why procrastination is dangerous, even if we can complete our tasks

Well, surely it's not too bad then, if all's well that ends well? We'll just focus our work at the last minute.

Unfortunately, it's not that simple! Procrastination is still a serious problem for several reasons:

- You can't always get there in time. Doing things at the last minute leaves a margin for error.

- It is not pleasant to have to solve a problem at full speed, with the pressure of having to finish in time.

- It does not allow you to shine. You have no time to reflect on an important task or improve your skills.

- It deprives you of the pleasure of doing important things in the long run. It limits you to small pleasures.

These effects sometimes go by unnoticed because we usually procrastinate small or medium tasks—but if you think you can do the same with important responsibilities, you will pay the price. Procrastinating has numerous negative effects on both you and your work. So then, let's see some consequences of procrastination.

The 5 consequences of procrastinating

Procrastinating is easy, fast and comfortable. It has two immediate benefits: extra time to dedicate to something else instead, and the relief of not having to do the more important task. But procrastination has its consequences.

Consequence #1: You accumulate more work

Within a few days, you'll see that you have not only the original task you postponed, but also new tasks that arose afterwards. Understandably, not many people will be willing to take time to help you with something that you've already postponed. Procrastinating a task will overwhelm you, and you'll have to carry the burden over the next few days. You therefore end up sabotaging yourself.

Consequence #2: You are more anxious

The more tasks you accumulate through procrastinating, the less time you have to address each one. This results in anxiety and stress. This state of mind is not good for you or the tasks you need to do, especially if those tasks require calm, concentration and a lot of effort.

Consequence #3: You have less time to prepare

Many tasks take time and cannot be improvised last-minute. Before you start, you need to be clear about your purpose, resources and planning, for example if you need to divide the task into parts. Preparation is vital, but you won't have time for that when you've left a task too late and accumulated other tasks.

Consequence #4: You do not allow for unforeseen circumstances

Important tasks are demanding and complicated, so they are not easy to finish. Sometimes unforeseen circumstances will change your situation or aspects of the task at hand. If you have procrastinated, you will have little or no time to deal with these changes, even if they become a matter of urgency.

Consequence #5: You lower the quality of your work

You need to complete your tasks to a certain standard and pay attention to detail. Sometimes you need to work to a very high level, especially if it is important for your studies or career. When you don't have much time, you are anxious, under-prepared and more rushed. As a result, your work will not reflect your best efforts, and this will be noticed by your professors, managers or clients.

In this chapter, we have seen the different reasons why people procrastinate and consequences of procrastinating. In summary, we can say that the worst part about procrastination isn't even the amount of work we have to do, but rather it's that we don't really feel good when we do it—no matter what our limbic system tells us. The cycle of delay creates feelings of guilt, anxiety, panic and tiredness. People who procrastinate become trapped in this stressful cycle and this turns it into a habit.

In the next chapter, you will learn more about how your performance is affected by your procrastination, and why actions taken to address the issue are often inadequate. But before we move onto the next chapter, it is important to remember that telling a chronic procrastinator to "just do it" is as unhelpful as telling a depressed person to "cheer up".

Chapter 2: Procrastination- A bad habit

Procrastination is a widespread habit that can be defined as the "kill-goals habit", even though the dictionary suggests it's more a matter of postponing or deferring your goals.

Unfortunately, the things we always defer tend to be "determining tasks". These tasks are important because they mark the difference between success and failure in all aspects of our lives.

Instead, we choose to do more fun but meaningless tasks. In most cases, these tasks simply do not serve any purpose, apart from consuming time—precious time that we could have used to advance towards our goals.

How procrastination affects performance

You may recognize the popular saying "do not leave for tomorrow what you can do today" (Count Phillip Stanhope in 1749/1968) and "nothing as dangerous as the procrastination" (John Lyly in 1579)

The habit of procrastinating and its consequences are quite common amongst people of all ages and sexes regardless of the type of activity. For example, in the educational field, studies carried out by researchers indicate that procrastination has a direct correlation with the academic results.

From this research, we can say that procrastination:

- has a direct negative relationship with academic performance,
- can be evaluated by using standardized tests to profile procrastinator students, and
- should be carefully considered by students faced with academic tasks, as part of regulating their own behavior.

But at the end of the day, there is no need to feel regretful or even hopeless. This is because procrastinators can learn to counter their bad habits by applying for specific training programs in procrastination management, which involves planning, time management, metacognition and affective-motivational strategies.

We should also remember that although procrastination is related to your own personality, this does not mean that it is an unchangeable part of you. That is to say, if you are considered a procrastinator, do not resign yourself to that label. Instead, think of it as an opportunity for personal improvement.
The solution is simple: you need to understand your personal procrastination situation, and you need to apply the right strategies to your procrastination habits.

There's only one thing left then: actually changing your habits.

Why it is difficult to stop procrastinating

Procrastinators have tried many different ways to stop procrastinating, but it never seems to work. Why is that? The answer is relatively straightforward: they do not attack the problem at the root. Imagine that you decide to prepare things in a different way. If you are a procrastinator, you will still find a new way to postpone things. You can diligently prepare to prevent this pattern from happening again, but what happens in the end? You still postpone the most important things again.

Now, excessive preparation may seem like a safe path. But when you get bogged down in details, you will still postpone necessary tasks again and again. There is no doubt that you are trapped in the cycle of procrastination. It seems like there is no way to escape. However, that is only because have been looking at this from a short-term perspective, instead of considering the long-term. So, how do you recognize when you are working effectively to stop procrastinating? How do you figure out how to target the root cause?

If you suspect that you fall into the same bad habits despite your efforts to stop procrastinating, try the following test. Answer the questions based on your usual behavior, and note the questions that reflect what you don't do. We'll see what the test tells us—then in Chapter 3, we'll share ways to avoid procrastination by attacking the root cause.

- Do you often second-guess yourself?
- Do you think you can rely on your intuition to make good decisions?
- Do you dodge productive actions whenever you feel tense?
- Do you have avoidable emergencies?
- Do you think you lack enough time to prepare for tasks?
- Do you think you need better organizational skills before you start tasks?
- Do you make important purchases on impulse?
- Do you avoid addressing emotional problems, such as anxiety?
- Do you delay as long as you can before you start things?
- Do you fantasize about doing things without much effort?
- Do you prepare yourself enough before taking on responsibilities?

Now, with your answers in mind, you will have a better understanding of why you procrastinate. It is essential for you to realize why you procrastinate before you move on. If you're ready for the next chapter, we will provide you with all the necessary tools to avoid and overcome procrastination.

Chapter 3: Tips to eliminate bad habits and create good ones

As we have said, procrastination can be both avoided and cured. One of the best ways to do that is to create good habits. Before we introduce the key solution (the 5 minute solution), it is important to read this chapter first. In order to ultimately overcome procrastination, you have to nurture positive habits instead of just implementing short-term actions. In this chapter, you will discover 3 positive habits that you should cultivate, as well as how to attack the root cause of your procrastination.

The 3 habits that you should nurture

Habit 1: Spend about 5 minutes planning your week.

Sunday night may be a good time to do this, though some people prefer to do this on Friday before the weekend. The actual day doesn't matter, as long as you set aside 5 minutes to do this. Try doing this on different days if you're not sure what suits you.

You should plan your week both professionally and personally, but also set aside time for yourself to simply do what you like.

Your personal tasks may include:
- The weekly grocery shopping and planning your meals.

- Booking and going to any medical appointments.

- Maintaining your home and addressing any technical household problems.

- Hobbies and leisure activities, including sports or outings with friends.

When considering your professional tasks:

- Organize your tasks in order of priority, from more to less urgent.
- Prioritize urgent tasks that you have to finish that week.
- Keep track of tasks that are in progress, but do not depend on you.
- Set yourself goals for that week and check them.

By the end of the week, you will see that you have achieved more than you think.

Habit 2: Eliminate distractions.

If you want to finish a specific task, do not be distracted by other stimuli.

Below is an example of how you can apply this method to a real scenario.

Imagine that you have several tasks to do:

1. Finish writing a document.

2. Prepare for a new project or assignment.

3. Submit an application.

You need to focus on these tasks and finish them all in less than 4 hours.

To help do this, you should:

- Put your phone out of sight, so you aren't tempted to keep checking it.
- Close all irrelevant programs and tabs on your computer.
- Avoid surfing the Internet, except if specifically required for a task.
- Avoid checking any social media.

Finally, allocate time to each task and keep to your deadlines:

1st hour: Finish writing the document.
Before moving onto the next task, reward yourself by making tea or having a treat.

2nd hour: Draft your plan and note important points for the new project.

When you finish, disconnect for 10 minutes by doing another task that you like more.

3rd Hour: Complete the application and submit it.
With your last half hour, you can answer any unread emails or messages.

Habit 3: Reward yourself for your efforts, but be flexible.

If you execute your tasks at a good pace, reward yourself afterwards. Take a short break before starting the next task—you can have a tea or coffee, or make a short phone call to a friend.

You can also reward yourself at the end of the day and again at the end of the week. You should decide what rewards are the best incentives to complete your tasks, as well as what your "punishment" is if you do not meet your daily or weekly goals.

Some examples are:

Incentives: Meet friends, go to the movies, buy something, go jogging.

Penalties: Ban yourself from using your phone or laptop for a short period of time, go jogging.

Depending on the person, jogging can be an incentive or punishment!

It is important to be flexible with ourselves, as we are not as motivated every day. Find the balance between the demands of your workload and what you can reasonably achieve.

Attacking the root of the problem

The best way to attack procrastination at the root is to design your tasks in a way that doesn't even leave a margin for it. Here are some ideas.

Idea 1: Choose your tasks well

If you systematically procrastinate in your studies or in your job, it is because you are not getting into the flow. And if you don't get into the flow—we're sorry to tell you, but maybe you're in the wrong subject or industry.

The flow has nothing to do with passion; it does not mean going through a whole day feeling uninterrupted. Instead, it is about selecting tasks that allow you to maintain a state of optimal concentration. If you are required by your studies or job to regularly do tasks that "violate your will", you are extremely likely to end up burned out.

Sure, you may say: "But I'm not going to change my degree or job to get into the flow. Could you give me more realistic advice?"

Of course, you don't have to put yourself in the radical mode of give-up-my-work-and-I-go-with-my-backpack. But the first step is to realize that the problem is not in you, but in the task and how it makes you feel.

Maybe this horrible task that you always procrastinate only gives you a very small benefit in your job or studies. Consider whether you can reduce the extent of the task somehow, eliminate it by delegating to someone else, or get the same task done in a different way.

Idea 2: Eliminate other "habitual suspects": perfectionism, burning out, etc.

It is worth considering that procrastination might be your friend and is here to help you. You may find that the underlying problem has nothing to do with motivation.

- Perhaps what it needs is to save you from your perfectionism, from your own belief that you are not enough, and to get you away from the risk of completing the task.

- Maybe it wants you to rest.

- Maybe it is here because you haven't spent enough time thinking about a good idea for your project, and now you're bored like a monkey.

In that case, the solution is not your willpower. The solutions are, in this order: abandon perfectionism, rest more and come up with new ideas.

Sometimes procrastination is your body telling you that you need to get away a little and think more about what you're doing. Don't stay in a loop in front of the computer, browsing Facebook non-stop and feeling guilty. Think. And then, act differently than how you have been so far.

Idea 3: Use deadlines

"Keep working and send it to me when it's ready." Alert, alert! If you have a tendency to procrastinate, then don't accept this from your professor or manager. Tell yourself this: "No, I'd rather set a deadline so I can organize myself better."

Pick a deadline and stick to it. Publicly commit to the person who needs you to complete the task: "I will have it finished for you on that day without fail."

Idea 4: Plan far in advance

On your calendar, find the dates for an important project and change them to one or two weeks earlier. Note the minimum time you'd need to do a good job, then when the time comes, start with enthusiasm.

But what if an unforeseen circumstance arises?

Remember, focusing on any project creates some chaos in the rest of our lives. It's inevitable and it's positive. It is not a question of maintaining balance, but of unbalancing in different directions.

So what do you do if an unforeseen circumstance arises? In 99% of cases, you will have the capacity to figure out how to reorganize your task. In the remaining 1%, the chances are that the seriousness of the unexpected does not really impact your final outcome.

Chapter 4: The 5 minute solution

As promised, we will now introduce the key solution of this book: The 5 minute solution.

It is essential that you implement the tips from Chapter 3 as well as this 5-minute solution, as together they serve as the fundamental idea for overcoming procrastination.

This strategy is fairly easy, so don't be surprised if you expected a more complicated description. Others have varied this little strategy to 2 minutes or 10 minutes. However, in this book, we will concentrate on habits you can create in 5 minutes

Most of the things that you procrastinate are in fact hard to do, because you have the talent and skills to complete them. You simply avoid doing the tasks for other reasons. The 5 minute solution tackles procrastination by making it easier to start each task.

There are three parts of the 5 minute solution.

Part 1: Whatever the task is, spend 5 minutes on it

What has proven most effective in overcoming procrastination is based on what is called the 5 minute solution.

So, instead of saying that you have to spend the whole morning working on a project or writing material for a marketing campaign, just start with 5 minutes.

If it's a phone call, pick up the phone and make the call. If you need to submit an article, write as much as you can in 5 minutes. Maybe your work will be brilliant or maybe it won't, but it doesn't matter; the fundamental thing is that you will have broken the cycle and shown that you can face stress.

That eliminates the main blow that procrastination throws at you. It is the psychological anxiety that makes you look at a task and only see how hard it will be.

Knowing that you're only going to be 5 minutes reduces that anxiety to a large extent, because it's such a small amount of time.

Where is the trick?

The trick of this technique is that your brain is lazy and also works a lot with inertia. If you're standing still, as is the case before getting on with the important task, you want to continue standing.

But if you overcome the initial inertia, then it's very likely that you might continue moving in the same direction. So if you start with 5 minutes, this will trigger a natural inclination to finish something you've started, and you will be pushed to continue beyond the 5 minutes—you can take advantage of one natural phenomenon to beat another.

Now, for this to work, it's important to avoid the intention that you might really take one hour instead of 5 minutes. You need to set a real goal of 5 minutes. If you then naturally want to continue, perfect! If not, nothing happens, move on, focus on something else. Later on, you can try another 5 minutes to see if this time you get hooked.

Part 2: Do a countdown of 5

When the time has come to do something, your instincts ignite. You know you have to do it, but you feel doubt. That is the moment when you have to do a countdown of 5 before you get going. This can be 5 seconds or 5 minutes, etc. If within 5 minutes you don't start doing what you need to, your brain will abandon the idea and you will convince yourself to leave it for another time.

Remember:
- The countdown must always be from 5: This simple action will give you a specific moment when you have to stop procrastinating and get going. This allows you to enjoy your procrastination first, then in 5, 4, 3, 2, 1 ... action!
- Act: Procrastinating and avoiding the inevitable are habits that will grow over time, becoming real burdens for your motivation and performance. Small daily victories are what give rise to win great battles. It's less painful to face those tricky tasks little by little than to confront them when they have become a big snowball
- Be brave: Procrastination is also the direct result of constant worry and negativity. You must first find the courage to do something in order to improve that situation

Part 3: Do tasks for 25 minutes and rest 5 minutes

The third part of the 5 minute solution is to improve productivity is based on doing a task across 10, 15 and 25 minutes, then resting for 5 minutes.

As an example, imagine that you have to prepare a business email that will take 25 minutes in total. You take between 10 and 15 minutes to write an email and then another 10 minutes to send it to a mailing list. Then you can take about 5 minutes of rest to talk with a friend on social media, watch the news, have a coffee or a tea, etc. Every 25 minutes, you should set small goals to reach. Each goal must include an objective with a 5 minute break.

We have discovered that this is the best mentality to apply, because if we set aside 5 minutes knowing that the task will really 50, then the psychological anxiety of the task is not reduced.

The physics of real life

We have long learned from Isaac Newton that all objects behave according to their initial form or according to the force that is applied to them, i.e., they can be at rest or in movement according to the force. This can apply not only to humans but also to falling apples.

The inertia of life allows you to understand the purpose of this 5 minute solution in life. You can apply that rule to any type of goal you have. The most important thing is to start. When you start, you will be able to keep doing it. This 5 minute solution is important because it adopts the idea that all good things happen once you start.

Do you want to create the habit of reading? Just read the first page of a new book, and before you know it you will have read the first three chapters.

Do you want to run three times a week? Every Monday, Wednesday and Friday, just put on your running shoes. By applying the rule, you will end up strengthening your legs instead of putting fried food in your stomach.

The most important part of a new habit is to start—not just the first time, but every time. It's not about performance, but consistently taking action. In many ways, starting is more important than succeeding. This is especially true in the beginning because there will be a lot of time to improve your performance in the future.

The 5 minute solution is not about the results you want to achieve, but the process of actually doing the task. This works best for people who believe that the system is more important than the target. The focus is on acting and letting things flow from it.

Try it now

We cannot guarantee that the 5 minute solution will work for you, but we can guarantee you that it won't work if you don't try.

This book has emphasized that procrastination can change from an annoying habit into a very serious problem. That is why we have to tackle the root of the problem by applying our tips and strategies. In order to overcome procrastination, you need to learn the 3 main habits and the 5 minute solution, then put them into practice.

The problem with most books, podcasts and videos is that you consume the information but never put it into practice. We want this book to be different. Use this information now. Is there anything you can do in less than 5 minutes? Do it right now.

Chapter 5: Additional tips- A simple plan to overcome procrastination

By now, most of you will have a much better idea about what to do to overcome procrastination. We would like to give you some more options to build on your thoughts.

Realistically, we understand that the tips in Chapters 3 and 4 may not be as helpful for some of you. Don't worry, this chapter was created just for you. Read on and you may find at least one tip that is just right for you.

Overcoming procrastination is not a matter of having a long list of tricks and strategies. In fact, if you want to stop wasting time and resolve your problems at once and for all, this chapter will give you a simple plan of action. Choose an option to start, then stop procrastinating.

To be successful, two ingredients are fundamental: the force of will and discipline, seasoned with a dash of motivation. Stop hanging around and follow this action plan to be more productive in your life.

Option 1: Make more immediate rewards

If you can find a way to make more immediate benefits for long-term goals, then it is easier to avoid procrastination. One of the best ways to feel the effect of future rewards early is by using a strategy known as the "cluster of temptation". This idea of grouping temptation was developed through research on the economy's behavior, conducted by Katy Milkman at the University of Pennsylvania.

The basic format is: only do [something you love] while doing [*something that you are procrastinating*]. Here are some common examples of grouping temptation:

- Listen to audiobooks or podcasts that you like while *exercising*.

- Watch your favorite TV program while *doing household tasks like ironing*.

- Eat at your favorite restaurant while *holding your monthly meeting with a difficult colleague.*

Option 2: Make more immediate consequences

There are many approaches that make you pay earlier if you postpone tasks.

For instance, on the off-chance that you are avoiding exercise, your wellbeing isn't immediately affected. The cost of deferring the activity just means that it gets more difficult after a long period of sluggish behavior. However, if you agree to go running with a friend at 7am next Monday, the cost of avoiding your exercise is more immediate. If you don't prepare, you will feel like a fool if you can't keep up.

Another option is to bet with a family member that you will exercise 3 days a week. If lose the bet, you have to pay them 30 dollars (this must be a set amount that is significant to you).

Option 3: Design your future actions

One of psychologists' favorite tools to overcome procrastination is called a "compromise mechanism". Compromise mechanisms can help you stop procrastinating by designing your future actions.

For example, eating habits can be controlled by buying food in smaller individual containers, instead of buying them in bulk. Or you can stop wasting time on the phone by removing some social networking apps. You can also build an emergency savings fund by creating an automatic transfer every month to your savings account.

These are just a few examples of compromise mechanisms that help reduce the odds of procrastination.

Option 4: Make the task more attainable

The stress caused by procrastination is usually focused around starting a task. After you have started something, it's less painful to keep working on it. This is a good reason to reduce the extent of your habits or goals. If your habits are small and easy to start, then you will be less likely to postpone things.

For example, consider the remarkable productivity of the famous writer Anthony Trollope. Applying this approach allowed him to enjoy the feeling of satisfaction and achievement every 15 minutes without failing to work on the great task of writing a book.

Extra: The Lee Ivy method

One of the reasons why it is so easy to fall back into procrastination is because we do not have a clear system to decide what is important and what we must work on first.

One of the best systems of productivity is also one of the simplest. It's called the "Lee Ivy method" and has 5 steps:

1. At the end of each working day, write down the 6 most important tasks you need to do to have a productive morning. Do not write more than 6.

2. Prioritize those 6 tasks.

3. The next morning, focus only on the first task.

4. Follow the list in the same way. At the end of the day, make a new list of 6 tasks for the next day.

5. Repeat this process for every working day.

This is what makes it so effective:

1) It's simple enough to get to work

Some criticize the method for being too basic, as it does not take into account all the intricacies and nuances of life, such as emergencies. While crises and unforeseen circumstances do arise, do your best to get past them and return to your breakdown of tasks as quickly as possible.

2) It forces you to make difficult decisions

There's no magical reason behind why we must choose exactly 6 important tasks. If you feel that 5 important tasks are sufficient for you, then try that. Regardless, we accept that there is something mysterious about applying limits to ourselves. When you are overwhelmed by an excessive number of thoughts or tasks, it seems like the best thing is to prune your thoughts and cut out anything that isn't essential. Confinements can improve you. The Lee Ivy method is like the "Warren Buffett 25-5" rule, which instructs you to focus on just 5 basic errands and disregard everything else.

3) It eliminates the stress of starting

The biggest obstacle for most tasks is how to start them. Getting up from the couch can be difficult, but once you really start running it's much easier to finish your workout.

4) It helps you focus on one task

Present-day society loves multitasking. The ideology of multitasking is that being busy is almost the same as being better. But this is the complete opposite of reality. Having fewer needs or responsibilities allows you to better focus on the task at hand. Look at any specialist of any subject (athletes, artists, scientists, teachers), and you will discover a common feature in all of them: the focus. The reason is simple. You cannot be great at a task if you are constantly dividing your time in 10 different ways. You need concentration and consistency.

Regardless of the method you use, the conclusion is the same: start with the most important task every day, and let the flow take you to the next.

As we said at the beginning of this chapter, there is not an exact list of tricks to stop procrastinating. There are action plans and different methods that you can apply. Choose whichever suits you. You can use one method, a combination, or none at all—you can implement solutions from Chapters 3 and 4 but skip Chapter 5. The only way to find out which method suits you best is to try them.

So, what are you waiting for? Adopt any of these methods now and you will soon find that one is bringing you closer to your goals.

Chapter 6: The 4 main benefits when you stop procrastinating

When you stop procrastinating, you will notice the vast benefits that follow. In this chapter, we will discuss the 4 main benefits that you may see after you start to overcome procrastination.

Benefit 1: For your studies

When it comes to studying, many people have distractions and choose to watch a movie, telephone their friend or go outside to avoid spending the afternoon studying. Sometimes we can afford an afternoon off; but when you actually stop procrastinating, you are more likely to improve your academic performance and have more control over your life. Procrastinating students intend to carry out the required task, but their brain instead decides to replace that with something easy and fun. Those who suffer from this usually have motivational problems, short attention spans, and are easily distracted—they do not know how to make the most of their capacity for paying attention.

If this sounds like you, create specific goals and ask someone for help to monitor you. Discipline yourself to face the tasks that you do not want to do, divide the tasks into small parts, and work to short deadlines. You will get better results, and little by little you will begin to change the bad habits into positive ones, allowing you to be one step closer to success.

Benefit 2: For your career

If you are a manager or leader, you usually instruct people to perform specific tasks and set deadlines for them. If the assigned people do not fulfill their obligations, you can hold them responsible and potentially use disciplinary measures. When you manage the schedule effectively, employees dedicate more of their working hours to important tasks, which can increase productivity and income for the company. When you handle the costs, you can also avoid unforeseen circumstances like fraud.

If you are an employee and try to stop procrastinating, you will be much more productive—you will finish the work you did before in much less time and at a higher standard.

The feeling of completing an assigned task can be more satisfying than all the congratulations of the world; it is something incomparable, as it has the advantage that you can keep doing that good work through conscientious preparation.

Benefit 3: Decreasing your stress levels

Once you stop procrastinating, you will have more free time— or at least you can finish your projects without rushing. When you handle your money well, you can worry less about how you're going to pay your expenses. Similarly, overcoming procrastination has the potential to reduce your stress level.

You will have more control over your life because you will know what you should do and when you will have extra time for yourself. You will be able to devote yourself to the things you like and not just the things you have to do.

This control translates to having less stress because when you have control over your time and your life, you immediately feel much calmer and relaxed.

Benefit 4: Productivity in your life

Consider the example of someone who procrastinates losing weight. In many cases, the solution is to keep a very strict diet so as to lose weight quickly. For a few months, the procrastinator can lose a lot of weight and feel motivated. However, a weight-loss diet cannot be maintained for too long because it isn't always healthy and requires discipline.

Personal productivity is exactly the same. Our task lists are overloaded with bad habits: procrastinating at work and not resting properly in our personal time. We are only interested in productivity techniques when we are overwhelmed. But it is important to realize that if we are constantly aware of the dangers of procrastination, we are less likely to fall back into the same habits; we need to have discipline.

Therefore, we shouldn't wait until we have too many tasks. Personal productivity is a way of understanding life, and helps us avoid taking on more than we can handle.

Conclusion

We have come to the last part of this book. After being exposed to so many tips, you might feel overwhelmed. To make things easier, we have come up with a helpful summary noting the most important 5 points.

To overcome your tendency to procrastinate:

(1) Learn to prioritize, because it is important to think about what things are most important in order to focus better.

(2) Schedule tasks in advance, by strategically organizing any outstanding tasks. You can make lists of tasks and activities in order of priority.

(3) Divide projects into steps, so that objectives are more likely to be fulfilled. For example, instead of losing 15kg, try 2kg at a time; or try writing a 500-page book in 15-page parts.

(4) Impose deadlines to finish things, so as to finish goals before starting other projects.

(5) Use rewards when goals are met, to nurture personal motivation and the desire for improvement.

Throughout this book, we have seen that procrastination is the habit of postponing necessary tasks and replacing them with activities that are enjoyable but unproductive. Procrastination can affect your studies, work, relationships and health; for example, if we avoid going to the doctor when we detect some troubling symptoms.

We have also seen that procrastination is commonly related to the anxiety of an outstanding task, and the lack of will to complete it. Our postponed tasks can be seen as challenging, dangerous, difficult or boring, so we might keep finding excuses to put them off until important tasks become urgent.

Chronic procrastination may lead to serious problems if it left uncontrolled. It occurs in all areas, regardless of the type of activity: studying at school, working at a job, having to do a medical procedure, doing the laundry or going to the gym. Procrastination is surfing the Internet or playing with your phone, while avoiding a necessary task.

However, do not despair, because we have the solution for you. In this eBook, we have provided you with steps, tricks, tips and finally a guide that will help you better organize your life. Remember, there's plenty of time.

If you have been a procrastinator for a long time, we suggest that you keep a journal of accomplishments. If it is a chronic problem for you, you need to do something to end the cycle.

Every day, write down instances where you don't end up doing what you need to, and explain why. If you do this every day, you will have a better understanding of your motivation to procrastinate.

These techniques work, but not if they are left in a drawer or on your hard drive. Use them, whichever methods suit you. Overcome procrastination because it is what gets between what you have now and what you want to achieve.

— *Magnus Muller*

About the author

Magnus Muller is a young writer who likes to explore the world as well as to play sports. He strongly believes that success can be attained with consistent hard work and effort.

He began writing his first book: **"The 5 Minute Procrastination Addiction Cure"**, to help those who suffer from procrastination to overcome it by just using a simple rule of thumb. He has now also published his second and third book: **"The 5 Minute To-Do List Formula"** and **"The 5 Minute Mindfulness Practical Guide"** to help his readers achieve their goals.

These 3 books come together to form "The 5 Minute Self Help Series". Since these 3 books are of different topics, hence you do not need to read them in chronological order but start with any book of your choice.

To find out more about his work, check out his books at **https://amazon.com/author/magnusmuller** and you will start to enjoy more free time and accomplish your tasks!

Leave a review

If you truly enjoy this book, please help to leave a review on Amazon! This book is now available in both the kindle and paperback version.

Kindle: https://www.amazon.com/dp/B07CT215ZZ
Paperback: https://www.amazon.com/dp/1983161640
Author: https://amazon.com/author/magnusmuller

The 5 Minute Self Help Series

The 5 Minute Self Help Series (Book 1)

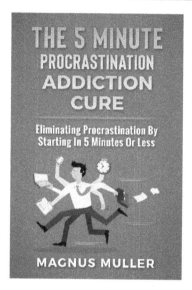

The 5 Minute Procrastination Addiction Cure
Eliminating Procrastination By Starting In 5 Minutes Or Less

By Magnus Muller

Kindle: http://www.amazon.com/dp/B07CT215ZZ
Paperback: http://www.amazon.com/dp/1983161640

The 5 Minute Self Help Series (Book 2)

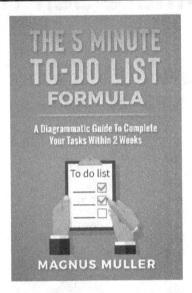

The 5 Minute To-Do List Formula
A Diagrammatic Guide To Complete Your Task Within 2 Weeks

By Magnus Muller

Kindle: http://www.amazon.com/dp/B07F8HFDLC
Paperback: http://www.amazon.com/dp/1983360260

The 5 Minute Self Help Series (Book 3)

The 5 Minute Mindfulness Practical Guide
20 Simple Habits To Lead A Stress Free Life, Reduce Anxiety And Treat Depression

By Magnus Muller

Kindle: http://www.amazon.com/dp/B07F8H6ZS2
Paperback: http://www.amazon.com/dp/1983360392

Check out other books

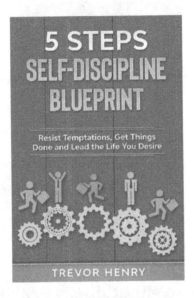

5 Steps Self Discipline Blueprint
Resist Temptations, Get Things Done and Lead the Live You Desire

By Trevor Henry

Kindle: https://www.amazon.com/dp/B07FLWHM3D
Paperback: https://www.amazon.com/dp/171778903X

Printed in the USA
CPSIA information can be obtained
at www.ICGtesting.com
CBHW020321161024
15908CB00035B/341